KLAL YISRAEL

OUR JEWISH COMMUNITY

BY ANN RICKI HURWITZ
AND SUE HURWITZ

BEHRMAN HOUSE, INC.

DEDICATION

TO RON
A.H.

TO GENE
S.H.

PROJECT EDITORS
ADAM SIEGEL, RUBY G. STRAUSS

DESIGNER
ROBERT J. O'DELL

PHOTOGRAPHY

Aron, Bill 86 / Berez, Isaac 47 / Byers, Richard 20 / Darmstaeder, Frank J. 8, 9, 17, 18 (top), 80 / Ernst, George 22 / The Jewish Museum 10, 11, 27, 11 / Joint Distribution Committee 48 / Kern, Robert L. 42 / Leffert, Sharon 36 / Stelman, Jacob 18 (bottom) / Sussman Photography 33 / United HIAS Service Inc. 57 / United Press International 74 / Wagner International Photos 53 / Wide World Photos 65, 72, 83 / WZPS Photo 77 / YIVO 10 / Zeiberg, Shirley 31 /

© COPYRIGHT 1991 BY ANN RICKI HURWITZ AND SUE HURWITZ
PUBLISHED BY BEHRMAN HOUSE, INC.
235 Watchung Avenue, West Orange, New Jersey 07052

ISBN 0-87441-511-X
MANUFACTURED IN THE UNITED STATES OF AMERICA

KLAL YISRAEL

OUR JEWISH COMMUNITY

THE BEGINNING OF OUR JEWISH COMMUNITY

People who are born in one country and then move to another are called immigrants. America is a nation of immigrants. Many people have moved here from other countries to build better lives for themselves and their families.

The Jews who came to America tried to re-create the communities they had left behind in their old homelands. They built the same kind of synagogues, formed the same types of organizations and often practiced the same professions that they had learned in Europe.

One of the first Jewish groups to arrive in America settled in New Amsterdam (the old name for New York). In 1645, they established a community modeled on the one they had left behind in Europe. They purchased land for a Jewish cemetery and met for prayers at each other's homes.

During colonial times, Jewish communities were established in the cities of Newport, RI; New York; Philadelphia, PA; Charleston, SC; and Savannah, GA.

Some Jews came to America during colonial times. This map indicates the earliest year that Jews were known to have lived in each of the original thirteen colonies.

According to the map, in which colony did Jews first settle? In what year?

Early mention of Jews in the Colonies

MASSACHUSETTS before 1649
NEW HAMPSHIRE 1693
RHODE ISLAND 1677
CONNECTICUT before 1659
NEW NETHERLAND (NEW YORK) 1654
PENNSYLVANIA 1734
NEW JERSEY 1718
DELAWARE 1655
MARYLAND 1656
VIRGINIA 1648
NORTH CAROLINA ?
SOUTH CAROLINA 1695
GEORGIA 1733
SPANISH FLORIDA
Atlantic Ocean
Gulf of Mexico
CUBA
YUCATAN
Caribbean Sea

W. Streckfuss

SCALE OF MILES
0 100 200 300 400

In 1730, early Jewish immigrants built a synagogue on Mill Street in old New York (pictured at left). The synagogue, which stood on Mill Street for over 100 years, was later rebuilt in 1818 (pictured at right).

Although there have been Jewish communities in the United States since the 1600s, most Jews living in America today are descended from immigrants who arrived here in the past 100 years. These immigrants were usually poor, arriving with little money and few belongings. They did not have the education or skills necessary to find good jobs.

Jews left their homes in Europe for the United States because they suffered from terrible discrimination and hatred. In Russia and Poland, Jews were not allowed to be citizens or to own their own land. The governments imposed special taxes on Jews to make sure that they remained poor and powerless. Sometimes angry mobs and government soldiers attacked Jewish villages. Because of these unbearable conditions, Jews moved to America, a land where they could be free to live and to worship as they chose.

COMING TO AMERICA

Between the years 1880 and 1910 2.5 million Jews came to the United States. Before Jews were allowed to leave their native country, they had to get their emigration papers approved. Jews in the German city of Bremen are shown standing on line at the steamship office, awaiting authorization for their emigration.

The voyage to America took two or three weeks. In order to keep kosher, Jews would often eat only bread, water and salted herring. One of the ways Jews maintained their sense of community during the long and dangerous journey was through daily prayer services.

Before immigrants were permitted to enter the United States, they underwent a thorough examination on Ellis Island in New York bay. In this photograph, taken in 1910, immigrants await inspection by the Immigration Bureau. Those immigrants considered undesirable were sent back to their homelands.

Arriving in New York was an overwhelming experience filled with relief. The long journey had come to an end. This Russian Immigrant, photographed in 1900, is ready to begin a new life filled with promise and hope.

THE JEWISH POPULATION IN THE UNITED STATES TODAY

Approximately six million Jews live in America today. On the chart, you will see the estimated Jewish population in each state and the District of Columbia. Look at the list and then see if you can answer these questions:

Which state has the largest Jewish population? _____

In which four states do the most number of Jews live?

_____ _____

_____ _____

Which state has the smallest Jewish population? _____

How many Jewish people live in your state?

_____

How many Jewish people live in your community. _____

State	Estimated Jewish Population
Alabama	10,000
Alaska	2,600
Arizona	69,200
Arkansas	2,000
California	868,200
Colorado	49,000
Connecticut	113,300
Delaware	9,500
District of Columbia	25,400
Florida	549,200
Georgia	62,500
Hawaii	8,000
Idaho	400
Illinois	259,800
Indiana	19,900
Iowa	6,700
Kansas	15,200

State	Estimated Jewish Population
Kentucky	12,200
Louisiana	16,800
Maine	8,800
Maryland	209,700
Massachusetts	286,600
Michigan	84,600
Minnesota	31,400
Mississippi	2,400
Missouri	63,600
Montana	450
Nebraska	7,300
Nevada	19,500
New Hampshire	7,000
New Jersey	427,700
New Mexico	6,400
New York	1,891,400
North Carolina	15,300
North Dakota	850
Ohio	136,000
Oklahoma	5,500
Oregon	12,500
Pennsylvania	347,000

State	Estimated Jewish Population
Rhode Island	17,500
South Carolina	8,300
South Dakota	450
Tennessee	19,700
Texas	97,800
Utah	2,700
Vermont	4,600
Virginia	65,300
Washington	22,700
West Virginia	3,300
Wisconsin	37,000
Wyoming	450

MY IMMIGRANT ANCESTORS

The people in your family who came from another country to live in the United States are your "immigrant ancestors." Perhaps you yourself are an immigrant. Who were the individuals in your family who made the decision to leave their homes and travel to America? Their decisions certainly had great impact on your life.

NAME _____

RELATIONSHIP TO ME

EMIGRATED FROM _____

PORT OF ENTRY _____

DATE OF ARRIVAL

AGE UPON ARRIVAL _____ PLACE OF SETTLEMENT

NAME _____

RELATIONSHIP TO ME

EMIGRATED FROM _____

PORT OF ENTRY _____

DATE OF ARRIVAL

AGE UPON ARRIVAL _____ PLACE OF SETTLEMENT

NAME _____

RELATIONSHIP TO ME

EMIGRATED FROM _____

PORT OF ENTRY _____

DATE OF ARRIVAL

AGE UPON ARRIVAL _____ PLACE OF SETTLEMENT

HOW DO WE HELP EACH OTHER?

One of the ways Jews have always helped one another is by doing *tzedakah*. The Hebrew word *tzedakah* means "doing the right thing." It means helping people who are not as fortunate as we are. It might mean giving money. It can also mean helping people find jobs or giving them an education or finding them a place to live. As Jews, we are obligated to perform acts of *tzedakah*.

One of the most important jobs of our Jewish community is to collect money for *tzedakah* and to see that it goes to help those who need it most.

In this book you will discover how our Jewish community is organized to do just that. You will learn how we fulfill our responsibilities to *klal yisrael* in our local communities, in Israel and around the world.

Tzedakah Box

We often put money for tzedakah in a special charity box. Sometimes this box is called a pushke. *Design a label for this tzedakah box for the charity of your choice. (Suggestions: Keren Ami, Jewish National Fund, Hadassah, Cancer Care, United Way, Operation Exodus.)*

II.
THE LOCAL JEWISH COMMUNITY

THE SYNAGOGUE

"Lord, You have been our
dwelling-place
in all generations."

(PSALMS 90:1)

This is the first line of Psalms 90. What do you think the author meant by the phrase "dwelling-place"?

A place to dwell is a place to live, like a home. But our rabbis believe that this Psalm does not mean an ordinary home, but the House of God. And that house, the rabbis teach, is the synagogue: "Our dwelling-place in all generations."

For more than 2,500 years, the synagogue has been the most important place in the Jewish community, a place where Jews gather to pray, to study and to celebrate happy occasions with one another.

Built in 1866, this synagogue named for Rabbi Isaac Mayer Wise, stands in Cincinnati, Ohio.

Synagogues come in all shapes and sizes. One of the earliest synagogues in America was built in 1795 in Charleston, South Carolina. The synagogue at the bottom of the page, designed by the modern architect Frank Lloyd Wright, was erected in Elkins Park, Pennsylvania.

FIND OUT ABOUT YOUR SYNAGOGUE

How well do you know your congregation? You can answer some of these questions by yourself. You may want to ask an older member of the congregation some of the others. Your parents can help you, too.

1 When did your family join the synagogue?

2 Why did your parents choose this particular synagogue?

3 What is the name of your synagogue?

4 What does the name of your synagogue mean?

5 How old is your synagogue?

6 Who founded it?

7 Who was the first rabbi?

8 What is the current rabbi's name?

9 How many families belong to the synagogue?

10 How many students attend the religious school?

11 Who is the principal?

12 What do you like best about your synagogue?

13 What *tzedakah* projects does the congregation sponsor?

THREE HEBREW NAMES FOR THE SYNAGOGUE

There are three Hebrew names for the synagogue. Each name tells us something about the synagogue.

Bet Tefilah means "house of prayer." This is probably how you think about your synagogue: a place where Jews come to pray together. Jews have always thought that it is better to pray together in a group than to pray alone. Some prayers can only be said if at least ten Jews (a *minyan*) are present.

Bet Midrash means "house of study." For hundreds of years, synagogues have been the center of Jewish education. Jews have always believed that studying our religion is extremely impor-

While we usually think of holding prayer services in a traditional building such as a synagogue, Jews gather to pray wherever they are. Here Jewish soldiers join together for outdoor morning services at a United States Army base.

tant. In fact, one of the *mitzvot* or commandments in the Torah is that every Jew must study the Torah throughout his or her whole life. Today, most synagogues have classes on Jewish subjects for everyone from children in nursery school to grandparents.

Bet Knesset or "house of gathering" is the third Hebrew name for a synagogue. This is the most common name for a synagogue and it refers to the synagogue as a meeting place. Jews gather at the synagogue for many reasons. Two reasons, to pray and to study, we have already discussed. But when we use the term *Bet Knesset*, we refer to all of the things that Jews participate in when they meet at the synagogue: cultural events, club groups, holiday activities, art and music programs and so forth.

A TOUR OF THE SYNAGOGUE

Mr. Samuels is the education director of a large synagogue in St. Louis, Mo., that has 1,500 members. As Mr. Samuels gives us a tour of his synagogue, think about how your synagogue compares with his.

"Welcome. Let's begin our tour in the main sanctuary where our members are seated for Shabbat and Holiday services.

"In front you see a large bimah, the platform from which the Torah is read. Hanging from the ceiling is the *ner tamid*, "the eternal light." Beneath the *ner tamid* is the *aron Kodesh*, "the Holy Ark." The Torahs are kept inside the ark.

"Now that we have seen the *Bet Tefillah* part of our building, let's go see the *Bet Midrash*. Follow me and I'll show you our school. Our students study two weekday afternoons and on Sunday mornings. We also have high-school classes, two nights a week for teenagers who have already become bar or bat mitzvah. Our high-school students study here for confirmation, which celebrates their graduation from religious school.

"We are now in the social hall of the synagogue. Right now the rabbi is encouraging members to help the new Russian immigrants in our community. Our Sisterhood and Brotherhood often sponsor meetings about important Jewish issues. They plan educational programs and work to raise money for *tzedakah* and to help support the activities of our synagogue.

Our synagogue is really like a home to the whole community. This synagogue may be different than the ones our ancestors knew in Europe, but it is still the most important place in the Jewish community. After 2,500 years, the synagogue is still the place where Jews gather to pray, to study and to celebrate. Shalom."

Can you find the bimah, the ner tamid and the aron kodesh in this picture?

SYNAGOGUE DICTIONARY

What do these words mean?

TZEDAKAH

BET MIDRASH

DWELLING-PLACE

BIMAH

PSALM

CONFIRMATION

BET KNESSET

NER TAMID

BET TEFILAH

ARON KODESH

SHALOM

MITZVOT

THE JEWISH FEDERATION

"Open your hand to the poor and needy among you...." DEUTERONOMY 15:11

Sometimes a single word can have several important meanings. Consider the Hebrew word *tzedakah*. Most people think of *tzedakah* as charity. But the word actually means righteousness. When Jews give charity, we do so not only because it is a nice or kind thing to do but because it is the *right* thing to do.

The Torah tells us to "open your hand to the poor." But deciding who should get *tzedakah* is not always easy. How do we know who really needs help? How do we know how much to give? And what is the best way to give? Are there other ways of helping people besides giving money?

These decisions are the responsibility of a very important community agency usually known as the Jewish Federation.

One who gives before being asked.

4

One who gives a proper amount after being asked.

3

One who gives less than is appropriate, but gives cheerfully.

2

One who is asked and gives unwillingly.

1

One who helps
people to provide
for themselves, so
they will not need
future help.

8

Both giver and re-
ceiver are unknown
to each other.

7

One who gives and
does know the re-
ceiver but remains
anonymous to him
or her.

6

One who gives and
does not know the
receiver.

5

EIGHT LEVELS OF *TZEDAKAH*

Maimonides, a famous Jewish philosopher,
classified people who perform acts
of *tzedakah* into eight groups. The eighth
level is, according to Maimonides, the highest
level of giving *tzedakah*. Do you agree?

TZEDAKAH SORT

How would Maimonides have rated these acts of tzedakah?
Write the number (1-8) next to each example.

_____ Sam spent his allowance to plant a tree in Israel
for his mother's birthday.

_____ Eugene tutored his classmate, a Russian
immigrant, in English so that he could do better
in school.

_____ Jessica cleaned out her closet and donated her
outgrown clothing to charity.

_____ Jeff and Nancy helped an elderly neighbor
to rake the leaves from her yard.

_____ Josh rode his bicycle in a bikathon
to raise money for muscular
dystrophy.

_____ Tali brought cans of food
to religious school for the
Thanksgiving food drive.

Can you think of other examples?

_____

_____

_____

_____

_____

_____

_____

In the early 1900s, most immigrant Jews settled on the busy streets of New York's lower East Side. Families lived in small tenement apartments and often spoke little or no English. Finding work and suitable health care was often very difficult.

THE STORY OF THE JEWISH FEDERATION

When Jewish immigrants came to America, they tried to re-create the communities they had left behind in Europe. They tended to live in areas with other Jews who came from the same place. They

formed groups to help one another. These agencies helped new immigrants find jobs and learn English and provided them with health care.

This system worked well enough when the community was small. The agencies knew who needed help in the community, and the people who needed help knew where to receive it.

But the agencies were not without problems. In order to give *tzedakah* to people who needed help, money had to be collected from members of the community. Often the different groups would compete with one another to collect money. This competition served to divide rather than to unite the Jewish community. In addition, the agencies had to spend more time raising money than they did helping people.

A special organization was needed to raise money. This organization would then distribute the money it collected to the individual agencies that worked with people who needed help. And that is how the Jewish Federation began.

Young immigrant girls learned to sew at the Jewish Manual Training School in Chicago, 1892.

One of the very first organizations that the various agencies formed, the Society of United Hebrew Charities, was organized in Philadelphia in 1869. Organizations like this one were formed throughout America and became known as "the Jewish Federation." In time, almost every community had its own federation to make sure that the agencies in its area received money to provide services to the people in the community who needed it. Just as the Jewish Federation in each town or city is made up of smaller agencies in that community, the various federations throughout America are united in a national organization called The Council of Jewish Federations and Welfare Funds.

While the Jewish Federation began as an organization to raise and distribute money to local agencies in the Jewish community, its primary function today is the distribution of funds it receives from the United Jewish Appeal/Federation Campaign. Money needed for local agencies, for Israel and Jews around the world is raised by the United Jewish Appeal (UJA). You will read more about this later.

What is a Jewish Community Center?

The Jewish community center (JCC) is an agency which receives funds from the Federation. It is an important place where Jews come together to build a community. In your city, the JCC might have a different name: the YM-YWHA. These letters stand for "Young Men's and Women's Hebrew Association." Often it is just called the "Y."

Most community centers have facilities for many different kinds of activities. The Y is a place for sports: there is a gym and a swimming pool. The JCC is a place for the arts: there is a theater and a gallery.

Another important JCC activity is education. Classes for all ages from nursery school to adult are offered. Usually, day-care centers for young children whose parents work during the day can be found there, as well as senior citizen centers where older people come to enjoy the company of people their own age.

Children celebrate Shabbat at the YM-YWHA summer day camp in Scarsdale, New York.

Made up of veterans from various Israeli wars, the Israel World Championship Wheelchair Basketball team played the Utica Wheels in a game sponsored by the Jewish Community Center.

THE JEWISH CENTER BULLETIN BOARD

NEED INFO ON TRIPS TO ISRAEL? GO TO ROOM 314

CHINESE COOKING LEARN TO COOK IN A WOK WITH EASY ORIENTAL KOSHER RECIPES

SUMMER CAMP BEGINS JUNE 22 DON'T FORGET TO GET YOUR APPLICATIONS IN EARLY!

JOIN US ON THURSDAY EVENINGS

ENGLISH CLASSES ON TUESDAY EVENINGS AT 7:00 RUSSIAN OUTREACH PROGRAM

JEWISH FOLK DANCE GROUP

JEWISH MUSIC CONCERT THIS SATURDAY NIGHT

VISIT THE ART GALLERY TO SEE PHOTOGRAPHIC EXHIBITION

SWIM TEAM BEGINS NEXT WEEK. SIGN UP NOW!

CONVERSATIONAL HEBREW CLASS GET READY FOR YOUR TRIP TO ISRAEL

TRY OUT FOR THE PURIM PLAY THIS WEDNESDAY AT 4:30 IN THE AUDITORIUM

Which announcement interests you most?

_____

HOW ARE JCCs DIFFERENT FROM SYNAGOGUES?

Some JCCs sponsor day camps and weekend trips for teenagers.

In some communities the Jewish community center and the synagogue are one and the same place.

Does your synagogue call itself a Jewish community center? If so, then it may not only have a sanctuary, a religious school and a social hall, but probably a gym and maybe even a swimming pool.

But some JCCs do not have a sanctuary. They encourage their members to pray at one of the synagogues in the community. Let's talk with the director of this type of JCC.

Mrs. Paley is the director of the JCC in Kansas City, MO. Kansas City has a Jewish population of about twenty thousand.

How did you decide to become a Jewish community helper?

"I love the Jewish community; I love the feeling of belonging to such a big family. Because I grew up in Kansas City, I am familiar with the needs of the local Jewish community. And most importantly, I have always enjoyed working with people."

What kinds of programs does your JCC offer?

"We sponsor all kinds of religious and cultural programs. We celebrate holidays like Hannukah, Sukkot, Passover, Lag B'Omer and Tu B'Shevat. We also hold Jewish song festivals and Israel Independence Day parades. We invite Israeli performers. It is important that we keep in touch with our fellow Jews all over the world. That is why we also have a Russian outreach program."

Please tell us about your Russian outreach program.

"As you know, many Russian Jews have immigrated to the United States in the past ten years. We provide English classes for Jewish immigrants from Russia and other foreign countries. We help these people get acquainted with other Jews in our community. We also help new immigrants find jobs and apartments.

We do this to keep *klal yisrael* strong."

YOU
BE THE
DIRECTOR

You are the director of a Jewish community center. You are in charge of planning the programs for the day. Be sure to include activities and programs for members of every age group.

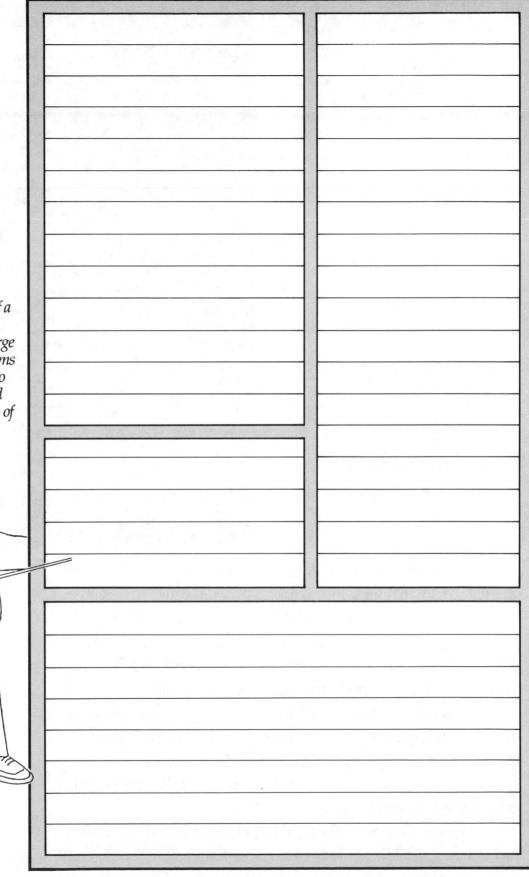

THE HOME FOR THE AGED

"Honor Your Father and Mother."

EXODUS 20:12

Some people live very long, active lives. They are able to live on their own when they are old just as they did earlier in their lives. Others don't age that easily, and it becomes difficult for them to live alone. They may need professional nursing care. Sometimes they can only receive the care they need by leaving home and moving to a place where doctors and nurses can take care of them.

This is when the larger family of the Jewish community assumes its responsibility. In many Jewish communities there is a Jewish home for the aged which provides care for those elderly people who can no longer care for themselves. The Federation helps to fund this important agency.

A Jewish home for the aged is more than just a place to sleep and to eat. A Jewish home tries to create a miniature Jewish community. Residents of the home eat together in cheerful dining rooms

Helping children learn to read is one way senior citizens remain active participants in the Jewish community.

where they enjoy the traditional Shabbat and holiday foods they have eaten all their lives. Most Jewish homes for the aged have a chapel with prayer books, prayer shawls and Bibles needed for services. Shabbat and holiday services are held in the chapel. Rabbis come to visit, conduct services and organize lecture or study programs.

Residents are still welcomed as part of the larger Jewish community. A minibus equipped with wheelchair lifts makes it possible for residents to attend community gatherings and synagogue services.

Jewish homes for the aged offer classes, discussion groups, musical programs and other events. But perhaps more important than all the activities that the home offers is the feeling it gives to senior citizens that they are still part of *klal yisrael.*

DECODE THE MESSAGE

Read each statement and decide if it is true or false. Circle the letter under the appropriate column.

TRUE	FALSE

1. Volunteer aides at a home for the aged help make the residents feel special.

2. Jewish homes for the aged conduct Shabbat and holiday services because they do not allow residents to leave the building.

3. Classes and musical programs are presented at the home for the aged.

4. Traditional Jewish foods are served in a Jewish home for the aged.

5. Residents of the home are forgotten by the members of the larger Jewish community.

TRUE	FALSE
H	W
R	O
N	C
O	J
T	R

Write the letters you circled to complete the sentence.

THE FIFTH COMMANDMENT TELLS US TO

_____ _____ _____ _____ _____ **OUR PARENTS.**

Andrew is in the tenth grade. During the summer, he works two days each week as a volunteer aide at the Jewish home for the aged. Andrew tells us about his work at the home:

"The days I work at the home are very important to me because my grandmother lives there. My family tried very hard to care for Grandma at home, but she needed more help than we could provide.

"When I arrive at my grandmother's room, she gives me a big hug. She asks about the family as I walk with her to the dining room for breakfast. Grandma misses us and I know that she looks forward to my visits.

"I take Grandma to her regular table where she usually eats with three friends. After telling Grandma I will be back to see her later, I start delivering meals to residents who are not as healthy as Grandma. I chat for a few minutes with each resident. Some of them are lonely and appreciate my visits.

"I usually save Dr. Solomon's tray for last so I can help him eat. He can't feed himself, so I'm there to help. I really enjoy talking to Dr. Solomon. We usually talk about sports, but I also learn a lot about history. He has all kinds of stories about how life has changed since he was a child. Dr. Solomon was born in Poland and moved to America when he was a child. Many of the people in my grandmother's home came to America when they were very small children. I think it's important to listen to Grandma and her friends because they have a great deal to tell us about life and traditions.

"After I deliver mail to the residents, I usually meet Grandma in the lounge with some of her friends. I play Scrabble or a card game with Grandma. Sometimes people ask me to read their letters to them.

"In the afternoon, Grandma often helps teach young children to read. The home has set up a program where the residents help tutor schoolchildren. The residents are still an important part of the community.

"When I say goodbye to Grandma, she always hugs me tightly and gives me a big kiss. She says goodbye and pretends to go back to what she was doing. But I know that she watches me until I am out of sight. I know that my visit made her day special."

WHAT CAN YOU DO TO HELP?

There are many things you can do as a volunteer at a home for the aged. Fill in the blank spaces to help you remember.

Older people enjoy hearing about _____. You

can bring a big bunch of fresh _____when you visit.

You can help them _____their hair or _____their shoes.

You can _____the newspaper aloud. Older people often have

interesting _____to tell. If you listen well, you might _____

something about the old days. Without visitors like you, a home for the aged

might get a little _____.

OTHER LOCAL AGENCIES SUPPORTED BY THE JEWISH FEDERATION

The following are just a sampling of the many other agencies supported by the Jewish Federation today.

The Jewish Family Service deals with many of the problems that people face. The agency offers counseling programs to help people with drug and alcohol problems. It helps families where the husband and wife do not get along or the parents and children fight a lot.

The Jewish Family Service often offers a "meals-on-wheels" program that brings food to people who are too ill or weak to prepare their own. The agency also has a telephone program in which volunteers call people who can't go out of their homes to make sure these people have someone to talk to. With the funds received from the Jewish Federation, the Jewish Family Service can help people regardless of their ability to pay.

The Board of Jewish Education (BJE) is an agency that provides support to Jewish schools. The BJE (often called "the Board" or "the Bureau") hires education specialists who give advice to the educational directors in religious schools. Some of the larger bureaus publish educational materials, but almost all keep a resource center where teachers and principals can view a wide selection of textbooks, videotapes, games and posters for Jewish classrooms. The BJE is committed to improving the quality of education throughout the entire community.

The Jewish Vocational Service helps unemployed people learn new skills so they can find jobs. The Service also helps students and young people find out what kind of professions they might enjoy and informs them about colleges and scholarship opportunities that are available to them. This agency often operates "sheltered workshops" for people who cannot work at regular jobs.

The Jewish Community Relations Council works to protect the rights of Jews and other peoples. The Council makes sure that everyone has equal opportunities in jobs and education as well as the right to practice one's religion. To help fight prejudice, the Jewish Community Relations Council tries to educate people in the general community about Judaism. They send speakers and educational materials to schools and organizations in the general community. They try to build better understanding between Jews and Christians in local communities.

The BJE helps teachers to decide which educational materials are best suited for their classes. At the BJE resource centers, where teachers are able to view a wide variety of textbooks, videotapes, games and posters, educational specialists offer advice on ways to improve the quality of education in classrooms throughout the community.

Ron's family recently moved to Baltimore from Canada. They are looking for a nursery school for Ron's baby sister so that his mother can look for work. Where should they go for help? _____

_____

_____

_____

_____

_____

_____

_____

Nancy is graduating from high school this year. She is having trouble deciding which college to attend. Where should she go for help? _____

_____

_____

_____

_____

_____

_____

_____

NAME THAT AGENCY

Adam's parents always argue. Adam has nightmares about all the screaming and yelling. He worries that things will never get any better at home and feels that he may be the cause of their problems. Where can this family go for help? _____

_____

_____

_____

_____

Jeff's classmates tease him because his family doesn't celebrate Christmas. His mother says that there is an agency in the community that might provide someone to speak to the class and give them the information they need. Which agency should she call?

_____

_____

_____

_____

_____

_____

In addition to the organizations we have described, the Jewish Federation supports local hospitals and Jewish schools. Some of the money raised also goes to agencies which help Jews in other parts of the world. The next time you give to the United Jewish Appeal/Federation Campaign, remember that the money you give helps to fund the agencies that improve the lives of Jewish people in your own community and all over the world.

III.
THE
NATIONAL
JEWISH
COMMUNITY

"How good and how pleasant it is that brothers dwell together." PSALMS 133:1

No matter where Jews live, we all belong to *klal yisrael*, the community of Israel.

You have read about some of the organizations that keep our local community healthy and strong. But what about Jews who live outside of your community? How do we maintain a connection with them? How do we keep our national Jewish community strong and healthy?

The hundreds of Jewish organizations in the United States not only help Jews in America, but also those throughout the world. Often members of different organizations come together for a common goal, as in the rally in front of the United Nations pictured here.

THE UNITED JEWISH APPEAL

One of the most important national Jewish organizations is the United Jewish Appeal (UJA). The UJA raises money to help Jews in America, in Israel, and throughout the world.

The United Jewish Appeal was founded in 1939 when many American Jews first realized that Nazi Germany planned to destroy all the Jews in Europe. Some of the European Jews managed to escape and come to America. Others went to Palestine ("Palestine" was then the name of the State of Israel). Money was urgently needed to help those Jews travel to Israel and to settle there. The UJA was formed to organize this collection of funds.

After World War II there were thousands of Jewish survivors who moved to Israel with hopes of rebuilding their shattered lives. After the end of the war and during Israel's War of Independence in 1948, the young State of Israel urgently needed the help of Jews around the world. The United Jewish Appeal helped the people of Israel create a new country.

The United Jewish Appeal has become the largest fund raising organization in Jewish history. Each local Jewish community runs a UJA campaign. About half of the money raised is used to meet local needs. The rest of the money is turned over to the National UJA for programs designed to improve life in Israel and to help our fellow Jews all over the world. Funds in Israel are administered by the Jewish Agency. The Joint Distribution Committee operates programs throughout the world for Jews in need.

From rescuing German Jews in 1939 to helping the Jews of Russia in our own day, the UJA has continued to reach out its strong hand to Jews all over the world.

THE NATIONAL COUNCIL OF JEWISH WOMEN

The National Council of Jewish Women (NCJW) is the oldest Jewish women's volunteer organization in America. Founded in 1893 by Hannah Greenbaum Solomon, it now has over one-hundred thousand members.

Since its earliest days, the NCJW has been devoted to upholding and securing the rights of women. In 1903 the organization formed a Port and Dock Department to help immigrant women who were arriving alone in the United States. In 1946 the NCJW opened homes in France and Greece for young women who had been victims of the Nazis. Areas in which the organization has played an active role include: equality of pay between men and women, prevention of teenage pregnancy, and the prevention of violence in the home.

One of the council's main goals is to improve the quality of life for children and youth. Members have provided aid to abused and neglected children and increased the quality of day care for children whose parents work.

The National Council of Jewish Women has been involved in over 2,000 projects from care for the elderly to assuring the freedom of speech and human rights for all Americans. Through a combined approach of social action, education and community service, the efforts of this organization have touched and transformed the lives of people of all ages, races and religions.

NATIONAL AGENCIES
THAT PROTECT
OUR RIGHTS

The **American Jewish Committee** and the **American Jewish Congress** are two other important organizations whose work insures the rights of the Jewish people.

The American Jewish Committee was founded in 1906 in response to the violent attacks on Jews in Russia at that time.

Throughout the following years, the Committee has worked very hard to end prejudice and discrimination against Jews in clubs, fraternities, colleges and businesses.

One of the goals of the Committee is to advance the cause of human rights for people of all races, creeds and nationalities.

The Committee is also working to see that Judaism is accurately described in the educational materials used in Christian religious schools. The Committee is devoted to dispelling myths about Jews that could lead to anti-Semitism. The Committee now has more than 40,000 members and offices in France, Israel, Mexico and South America as well as in the United States.

The American Jewish Congress was organized in 1918, twelve years after the American Jewish Committee. The original goal of the Congress was to help the millions of Jews in Europe who were trapped between the armies fighting the First World War. Later, during the Second World War, the Congress became one of the first American groups to understand the terrible danger facing Jews who lived under the rule of Nazi Germany. The Congress worked hard to educate other Americans about the Nazi threat.

More recently, the Congress has tried to eliminate racial and religious prejudice in the United States. Jews of all ages and backgrounds supported the Congress when it demonstrated for the rights of blacks during the Civil Rights Movement of the 1950s and 1960s.

In the 1960s, members of the American Jewish Congress rallied on New York's Fifth Avenue to demonstrate their support of the desegregation of lunch counters in Woolworth stores.

B'NAI B'RITH

B'nai B'rith, which means "sons of the covenant," was founded in New York City in 1843. This organization was designed to unite the members of the many new synagogues that were springing up across America and Canada. Members of different synagogues formed a group based on the ethical teachings of Judaism to promote peace and brotherhood among all peoples.

In the words of the founding fathers, "B'nai B'rith has taken upon itself the mission of uniting persons of the Jewish faith . . . of supporting science and art; alleviating the wants of the poor and needy; visiting and attending the sick; coming to the rescue of victims of persecution; providing, protecting and assisting the widow and orphan on the broadest principles of humanity."

B'nai B'rith pursues its goal of peace and brotherhood by

This building in Washington, D.C. (right), houses the Four Freedoms Library (below), which includes books on all aspects of human rights and the national offices of B'nai B'rith.

A
Directory
of
B'nai B'rith
Hillel Foundations
And Other Jewish
Campus Agencies

JEWISH

LIFE

ON CAMPUS

Published by
B'nai B'rith Hillel Foundations

The B'nai B'rith Hillel Foundation publishes a directory of Jewish activities on college campuses.

sponsoring youth activities, Jewish education for adults and Hillel Houses on college campuses. Hillel Houses give Jewish college students a place to worship and to organize Jewish events on campus. B'nai B'rith members also do volunteer work, helping people in local communities.

B'nai B'rith supports the Anti-Defamation League. This organization makes sure that American Jews and other minority groups are treated fairly. The Anti-Defamation League is a national organization that fights prejudice and injustice throughout the United States and Canada.

Today there are more than five-hundred thousand members in B'nai B'rith. Can you see why the motto of B'nai B'rith is "Alone I am weak; in B'nai B'rith I am tens of thousands strong"?

OTHER NATIONAL JEWISH ORGANIZATIONS

There are so many national Jewish organizations that it would take more than forty pages to list them all. Here are some of them. How many do you know?

ORT (ORGANIZATION FOR REHABILITATION THROUGH TRAINING)
Provides vocational/technical education to over 158,000 students at ORT schools in eighteen countries.

HIAS (HEBREW IMMIGRANT AID SOCIETY)
Assists Jewish migrants and refugees from Eastern Europe, the Middle East, North Africa and Latin America.

Due to the efforts of HIAS, the first 800 former inmates of Europe's liberated concentration camps arrived in New York on May 20, 1946 aboard the S.S. Marine Flasher.

JEWISH WAR VETERANS
Fosters allegiance to the United States and the education of ex-servicemen and women.

AMERICAN JEWISH HISTORICAL SOCIETY
Collects and publishes material on the history of Jews in America.

JEWISH BRAILLE INSTITUTE OF AMERICA
Serves the religious, cultural and educational needs of the Jewish blind and visually impaired.

NATIONAL CONFERENCE ON SOVIET JEWRY
Acts on behalf of Russian Jewry through public education and social action.

NATIONAL FOUNDATION FOR JEWISH CULTURE
Provides consultation and support to community organizations and educational institutions for Jewish cultural activities.

JWB (JEWISH WELFARE BOARD)
Leadership agency for North American network of Jewish community centers and Ys.

YIVO INSTITUTE FOR JEWISH RESEARCH
Engages in research pertaining to East European Jewish life.

PIONEER WOMEN/NA'AMAT
Provides social, educational and legal services for women and children in Israel and advocates legislation for women's rights and child welfare in the United States.

Encouraged by The Jewish Braille Institute, young people become involved Jews, and many become highly skilled professionals in medicine, law, teaching and Jewish communal work.

Helping BLIND JEWISH CHILDREN build their futures

The YIVO Institute for Jewish Research on Fifth Avenue in New York.

At the end of World War I in 1919, many Jewish communities in Europe were on the verge of famine. The Joint Distribution Committee organized food shipments from the United States to Europe. In this historic photo, rabbis are shown blessing the first shipment of kosher meat sent to the starving Jews of Poland.

A Seder at sea. Onboard the ship USS Puget Sound, a rabbi lights the festival candles as the Passover seder begins. Passover supplies for the seder—which took place as the ship traveled from Italy to Spain—were supplied by the Navy with the help of the JWB in New York.

AMERICAN JEWISH JOINT DISTRIBUTION COMMITTEE
Organizes and finances rescue, relief and rehabilitation programs for Jews overseas.

JESNA (JEWISH EDUCATION SERVICE OF NORTH AMERICA)
Coordinating, planning and service agency for Jewish education in bureaus and federations.

ORGANIZATION GOALS

Match each organization with its goal.

B'NAI B'RITH

AMERICAN JEWISH COMMITTEE

THE UNITED JEWISH APPEAL

ORGANIZATIONS

AMERICAN JEWISH CONGRESS

ORT

HIAS

GOALS

1
ADVOCATE PEACE AND BROTHERHOOD

2
SEEKS HUMAN RIGHTS FOR PEOPLE OF ALL RACES, CREEDS AND NATIONALITIES

3
ASSIST JEWISH REFUGEES

4
PROVIDES VOCATIONAL/ TECHNICAL EDUCATION

5
COLLECT AND PUBLISH MATERIAL ON JEWISH AMERICAN HISTORY

6
HELP ELIMINATE RACIAL AND RELIGIOUS PREJUDICE

7
RESCUE AND PROVIDE RELIEF FOR JEWS OVERSEAS

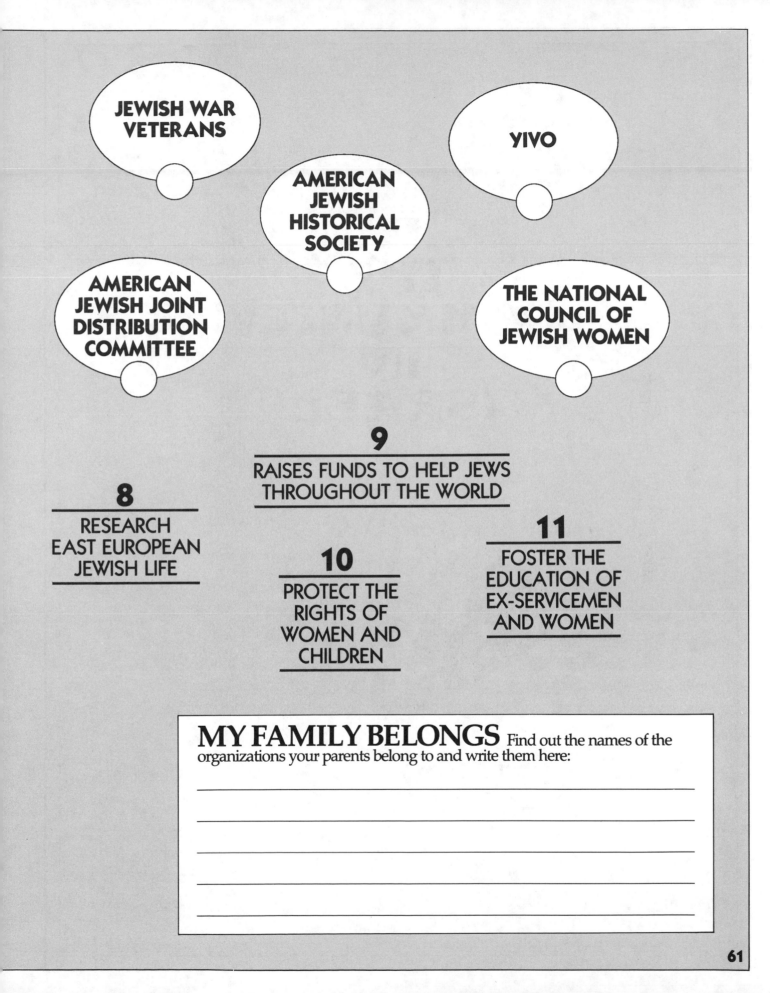

JEWISH WAR
VETERANS

YIVO

AMERICAN
JEWISH
HISTORICAL
SOCIETY

AMERICAN
JEWISH JOINT
DISTRIBUTION
COMMITTEE

THE NATIONAL
COUNCIL OF
JEWISH WOMEN

9
RAISES FUNDS TO HELP JEWS
THROUGHOUT THE WORLD

8
RESEARCH
EAST EUROPEAN
JEWISH LIFE

10
PROTECT THE
RIGHTS OF
WOMEN AND
CHILDREN

11
FOSTER THE
EDUCATION OF
EX-SERVICEMEN
AND WOMEN

MY FAMILY BELONGS Find out the names of the
organizations your parents belong to and write them here:

_____

_____

_____

_____

_____

IV.
THE
COMMUNITY
IN
ISRAEL

"A land that flows with milk and honey...." DEUTERONOMY 11:9

 he State of Israel, *Eretz Yisrael*, is very important in the lives of Jews around the world. We celebrate Israel Independence Day at our synagogues, religious schools and Jewish community centers. Our parents donate money and volunteer their time to the United Jewish Appeal. We pay special attention to news about Israel in newspapers and on television. What makes Israel so important to us?

For over 2,000 years, the small country of Israel has captivated the minds and hearts of Jews around the world. Can you list the five Arab countries that surround Israel?

1 _____

2 _____

3 _____

4 _____

5 _____

Beirut
LEBANON
SYRIA
Damascus
GOLAN HEIGHTS
Safed
SEA OF GALILEE
Haifa
MEDITERRANEAN SEA
Tel Aviv
Jordan R.
WEST BANK
Amman
Jerusalem
Gaza
DEAD SEA
Hebron
Port Said
Beersheba
ISRAEL
Suez Canal
NEGEV DESERT
JORDAN
Cairo
Suez
SINAI PENINSULA
Nile R.
Elat
Aqaba
EGYPT
GULF OF SUEZ
SAUDI ARABIA
STRAIT OF TIRAN

WHY ISRAEL IS IMPORTANT

Ever since the days of our biblical ancestor Abraham some 4,000 years ago, Jews have thought of *Eretz Yisrael* as their homeland. We read about Abraham in the Torah. He left the land of Mesopotamia and came to Israel. The Torah tells us that God promised *Eretz Yisrael* to Abraham and his descendants, the Jewish people.

In return, Abraham promised that he and his family, which includes us, would worship God, study God's teachings and obey God's commandments. Many times during our history Jews have been forced to leave *Eretz Yisrael*. Almost 2,000 years ago, after the Romans conquered Israel and destroyed Jerusalem, they sent the Jews into exile. Over the years we have established communities in almost every country in the world!

But wherever Jews have gone, we have not forgotten our ties to the Land of Israel. Our prayers and customs and even some of the special foods we eat remind us of Israel. The final words we recite at the Passover Seder, "next year in Jerusalem," show our deep and continuous connection to our homeland.

THINGS I DO THAT REMIND ME OF ISRAEL

Which holidays remind you of Israel?

What do you do on those holidays?

What do you do at synagogue that reminds you of Israel?

What foods remind you of Israel?

Are there any objects in your home that remind you of Israel?

The Declaration of Independence of the newly created State of Israel was read by David Ben-Gurion on May 14, 1948. Ben-Gurion would serve as the Jewish state's prime minister for the next 15 years.

Look at the picture hanging above Ben-Gurion's head. Do you know who that person is? When you have finished this chapter, you will not only know who he is but also why his picture serves as the centerpiece for this historic meeting.

WHAT IS ZIONISM?

There have always been Jews living in *Eretz Yisrael*. For a time however, the Jewish community in Israel was small and weak. Then, about 100 years ago, the community began to grow. Settlers came from Europe to rebuild the Jewish land. Many of these settlers were followers of a new movement called Zionism.

A Zionist is a person who believes that Jews should rebuild their homeland in *Eretz Yisrael*. The word Zionism comes from the Hebrew word Zion, which is another name for the city of Jerusalem.

Zionism has been one of the most successful political movements of the twentieth century. Over the years, the settlers built homes, farms, roads, towns and cities throughout *Eretz Yisrael*. Before long they had built an entire country. That country is the State of Israel.

ZIONIST ORGANIZATIONS

The founder of modern Zionism was an Austrian Jew named Theodor Herzl. In the late 1880s he formed the World Zionist Organization (WZO). Herzl brought together Jewish leaders from around the world and convinced them to work together for a Jewish homeland in Israel. Today, the WZO is the largest Jewish organization in the world. It coordinates activities throughout the world on behalf of Israel. In addition, the WZO encourages and supports *aliyah,* immigration to Israel.

The Jewish National Fund (JNF) is the fund-raising branch of the WZO. The JNF was formed in the early 1900s when large numbers of Jewish immigrants began coming to *Eretz Yisrael.* The JNF raised

Dr. Theodor Herzl was the founder of the Zionist Movement. In 1897, after the meeting of the First Zionist Congress which Herzl organized, he wrote in his diary, "Today I created the Jewish State. In five years, perhaps, and certainly in fifty, everyone will see it." Exactly fifty years later in 1947 the United Nations voted to create the State of Israel.

Do you remember seeing Theodor Herzl's picture somewhere else in this chapter?

Israeli farmers use plastic sheeting to grow fruits and vegetables in dry soil. Land that is fit for growing crops is created in Israel through the efforts of the JNF.

Trees are planted in Israel to remember important people and events. What will this forest commemorate?

money to buy land in Israel. This money was also used to drain swamps and irrigate deserts so the Jewish pioneers in Israel could farm the land. Today, the JNF continues to prepare the land of Israel for new housing, schools and industry.

The JNF has planted more than 160 million trees in Israel. These trees keep the soil from washing away on hills. They also provide shade and beauty, and they help improve Israel's defenses by acting as natural obstacles. On Tu B'Shevat, when your religious school asks you to plant a tree in Israel, remember that every tree we plant makes a difference.

MAKING A DIFFERENCE

One of the ways the Jewish National Fund strives to improve the land of Israel is through planting trees. List the different ways that trees help the country and the people who live there.

_____

_____

_____

_____

_____

_____

Theodor Herzl and Henrietta Szold were instrumental in creating and shaping the Land of Israel. Below are the beginnings of two sentences that each person might have spoken. Complete the statements of these people based on what you have read in this chapter.

"I helped build and strengthen the community of Israel by. . . ."

building hos-
pitals and giving
women a chance
to talk to each
other and be
Jewish. Also I
got doctors and
nurses to
help us.

"I helped create the State of Israel by. . . ."

creating a Zionist
organization for
people to
have the
land of
Israel and
persuading people
to get land.

Water has been flowing through the pipelines of the National Water Carrier since 1964. This photograph shows the construction of one of the waterline's tunnels.

THE ISRAEL BOND ORGANIZATION

The Israel Bond Organization was established in 1951 on the third anniversary of Israel's independence. Since then, ten billion dollars have been loaned to Israel through the sale of Israel Bonds. This money has helped to expand and to develop Israel's economy by paying for highways and apartments, for satellite ground stations to improve communications and for the National Water Carrier.

The National Water Carrier is a huge water pipe that brings water from the Sea of Galilee in the north down the whole length of the country. The water irrigates 450,000 acres of farmland so Israeli farmers can grow food to feed the country's people and to export to other countries.

HADASSAH

Hadassah is a Women's Zionist organization founded in 1912 by Henrietta Szold. Hadassah educates American women about Judaism and improves public health services in Israel.

Henrietta Szold devoted her entire life to the Zionist cause of reestablishing a Jewish homeland in Palestine. She was born in Baltimore in 1860 to a family of immigrants from Hungary. Although she grew up at a time when most Jewish girls did not receive much education, Henrietta studied long hours with her father, a rabbi, and she became a teacher at a night school for new immigrants to the United States.

In 1909, Henrietta Szold traveled to *Eretz Yisrael*. She fell in love with the land and its people, but the poverty and poor health care upset her. When she returned to the United States, she began organizing a group to promote better health care there.

Hadassah was founded in 1912 and two short years later had over 4,000 members. That same year, Hadassah organized the American Zionist Medical Unit consisting of doctors, nurses, administrators and ambulances. The unit arrived in 1918 and did a great deal to improve the health of immigrants in Israel. Today, Hadassah has 385,000 members and operates a network of modern hospitals throughout Israel, five of which are in Jerusalem.

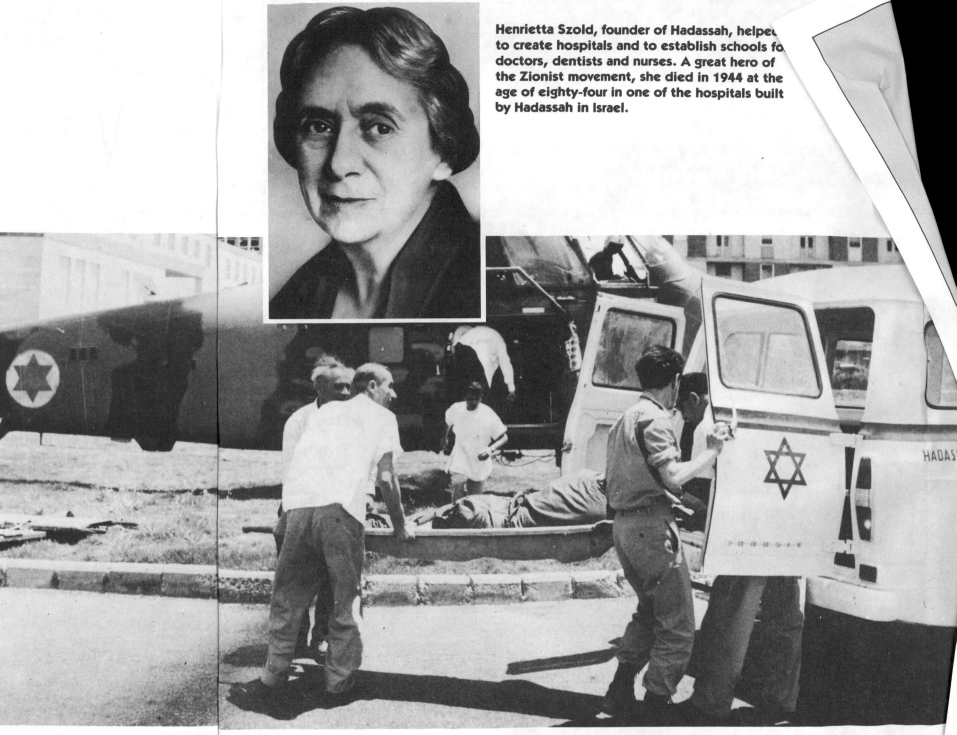

Henrietta Szold, founder of Hadassah, helped to create hospitals and to establish schools for doctors, dentists and nurses. A great hero of the Zionist movement, she died in 1944 at the age of eighty-four in one of the hospitals built by Hadassah in Israel.

A wounded soldier is flown by helicopter to a Hadassah ambulance.

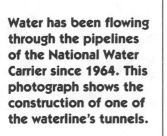

Water has been flowing through the pipelines of the National Water Carrier since 1964. This photograph shows the construction of one of the waterline's tunnels.

THE ISRAEL BOND ORGANIZATION

The Israel Bond Organization was established in 1951 on the third anniversary of Israel's independence. Since then, ten billion dollars have been loaned to Israel through the sale of Israel Bonds. This money has helped to expand and to develop Israel's economy by paying for highways and apartments, for satellite ground stations to improve communications and for the National Water Carrier.

The National Water Carrier is a huge water pipe that brings water from the Sea of Galilee in the north down the whole length of the country. The water irrigates 450,000 acres of farmland so Israeli farmers can grow food to feed the country's people and to export to other countries.

HADASSAH

Hadassah is a Women's Zionist organization founded in 1912 by Henrietta Szold. Hadassah educates American women about Judaism and improves public health services in Israel.

Henrietta Szold devoted her entire life to the Zionist cause of reestablishing a Jewish homeland in Palestine. She was born in Baltimore in 1860 to a family of immigrants from Hungary. Although she grew up at a time when most Jewish girls did not receive much education, Henrietta studied long hours with her father, a rabbi, and she became a teacher at a night school for new immigrants to the United States.

In 1909, Henrietta Szold traveled to *Eretz Yisrael*. She fell in love with the land and its people, but the poverty and poor health care upset her. When she returned to the United States, she began organizing a group to promote better health care there.

Hadassah was founded in 1912 and two short years later had over 4,000 members. That same year, Hadassah organized the American Zionist Medical Unit consisting of doctors, nurses, administrators and ambulances. The unit arrived in 1918 and did a great deal to improve the health of immigrants in Israel. Today, Hadassah has 385,000 members and operates a network of modern hospitals throughout Israel, five of which are in Jerusalem.

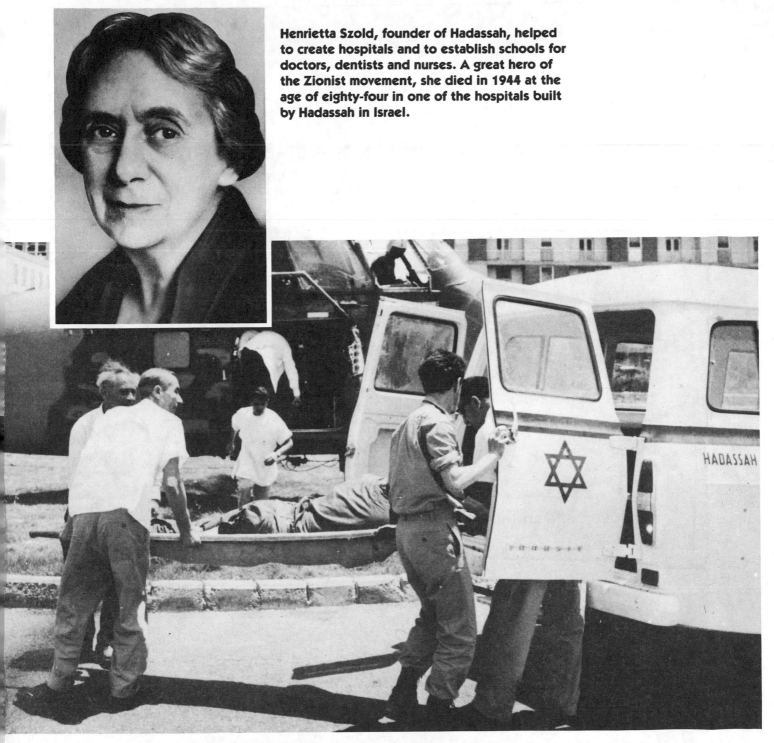

Henrietta Szold, founder of Hadassah, helped to create hospitals and to establish schools for doctors, dentists and nurses. A great hero of the Zionist movement, she died in 1944 at the age of eighty-four in one of the hospitals built by Hadassah in Israel.

A wounded soldier is flown by helicopter to a Hadassah ambulance.

Theodor Herzl and Henrietta Szold were instrumental in creating and shaping the Land of Israel. Below are the beginnings of two sentences that each person might have spoken. Complete the statements of these people based on what you have read in this chapter.

"I helped build and strengthen the community of Israel by. . . ."

building hos-
pitals and giving
women a chance
to talk to each
other and be
Jewish. Also I
got doctors and
nurses to
help us.

"I helped create the State of Israel by. . . ."

creating a Zionist
organization for
people to
have the
land of
Israel and
persuading people
to get land.

YOUTH ALIYAH

In 1933, Henrietta Szold founded a new organization called Youth Aliyah that encourages and helps young Jews to live in *Eretz Yisrael*. Youth Aliyah began its work by helping Jewish children escape from Europe before and during World War II. By 1948, 30,000 children mostly from Germany, had been rescued by Youth Aliyah and brought safely to Israel.

Youth Aliyah continues its work today by training young immigrants in Israel for new jobs. It also maintains special centers for emotionally disturbed children and works very closely with Hadassah to provide health care for young people.

A great hero of the Zionist movement, Henrietta Szold spent her life strengthening *klal yisrael*.

WORD MATCH

Match each person, place, or organization with its correct description.

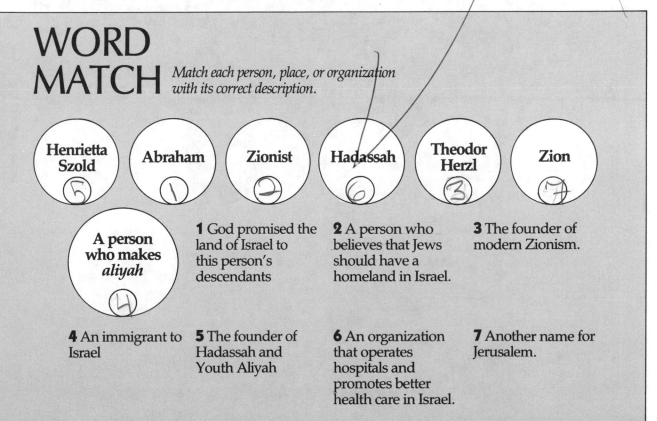

Henrietta Szold — 5
Abraham — 1
Zionist — 2
Hadassah — 6
Theodor Herzl — 3
Zion — 7

A person who makes *aliyah* — 4

1 God promised the land of Israel to this person's descendants

2 A person who believes that Jews should have a homeland in Israel.

3 The founder of modern Zionism.

4 An immigrant to Israel

5 The founder of Hadassah and Youth Aliyah

6 An organization that operates hospitals and promotes better health care in Israel.

7 Another name for Jerusalem.

A SPECIAL PARTNERSHIP

Throughout the world there are many different Jewish communities. But among all of the world's Jewish communities, there is only one Jewish country. There is only one place where Jews form the majority of the citizens. There is only one Israel.

Because Israel is so special, a partnership has grown up between our American Jewish community and the Jewish community of Israel. The Jews of *Eretz Yisrael* do all they can to build and protect our Jewish homeland. And we American Jews do all we can to support them.

Our two communities are the largest Jewish communities in the world. It is up to all of us to keep *klal yisrael* strong and healthy.

On May 7, 1978, 200,000 people paraded along New York's Fifth Avenue in celebration of Israel's thirtieth anniversary, as witnessed by this young observer.

V.
THE WORLD
JEWISH
COMMUNITY

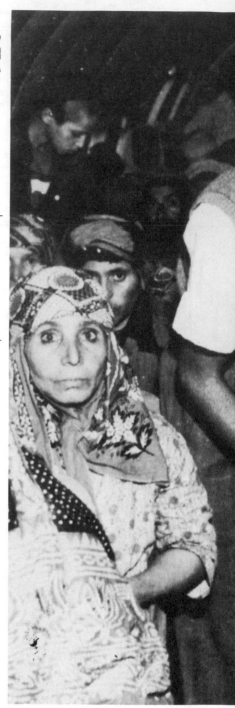

"All Jews are responsible for one another." TALMUD

Only one-fourth of the Jewish people in the world today live in the State of Israel. The Jewish communities outside of Israel are known as the *Diaspora,* from an old Greek word meaning "dispersion." Our Jewish community here in North America, which is part of this community of *Diaspora* Jews, is the largest in the world. Other large *Diaspora* communities are found in France, England, Argentina, Brazil, South Africa, Australia and Russia. Jews, no matter where we live, are part of *klal yisrael,* the community of Israel.

Many Jewish people outside of North America and Israel live and worship freely. Unfortunately, thousands of others are not free to do so. They live in countries where Jews are not allowed to practice their religion. They face persecution and discrimination. This is especially true of the Jews who live in Russia and in Ethiopia.

The Jews of Yemen suffered under an oppressive government for hundreds of years. Before 1948 some Yemenite Jews traveled to the land of Israel to escape the difficult conditions in their homeland. But it was the creation of the State of Israel which finally freed the Jews of Yemen. In 1950, the Israelis brought almost the entire Jewish population of Yemen to Israel, approximately forty-three thousand people! They were flown in large airplanes in a project called "Operation Magic Carpet." Today, Yemenite Jews are an important part of the culture and society of Israel.

JEWS ACROSS THE WORLD

Directions: Using the world Jewish population chart below, answer the questions at the bottom of the page. Then fill in the bar graph with the Jewish population of each country. Each square on the graph is equal to 500,000 people.

	POPULATION OF ENTIRE COUNTRY	JEWISH POPULATION OF COUNTRY
EGYPT	49,609,000	200
ETHIOPIA	44,927,000	12,000
FRANCE	55,392,000	530,000
IRAN	45,914,000	22,000
ISRAEL	4,333,100	3,562,000
JAPAN	120,492,000	1,000
POLAND	37,456,000	4,400
USA	241,596,000	5,700,000
CANADA	25,612,000	310,000

1. Which country has the largest population?

_____

2. Which country has the largest Jewish population?

_____

3. Which country has the second largest Jewish population?

_____

4. Which country has the smallest population?

_____

5. Which country has the smallest Jewish population?

_____

POPULATION OF WORLD JEWRY

	7,500,000
	7,000,000
	6,500,000
	6,000,000
	5,500,000
	5,000,000
	4,500,000
	4,000,000
	3,500,000
	3,000,000
	2,500,000
	2,000,000
	1,500,000
	1,000,000
	500,000

USA   ISRAEL   CANADA   FRANCE   IRAN   ETHIOPIA   POLAND   JAPAN   EGYPT

THE JEWISH COMMUNITY OF ETHIOPIA

Ethiopia is a country located in the middle of Africa. Ethiopian Jews are members of one of the oldest Jewish communities outside of *Eretz Yisrael*. They have lived in Ethiopia for over 2,000 years.

For hundreds of years the Ethiopian Jews had a proud history, but changing political conditions in their country have made life very hard for them. For many years there has been hunger and disease in Ethiopia caused by droughts, famines and civil war. In 1974, a new government took control of Ethiopia. It looked upon the Ethiopian Jews as foreigners and began an official program of persecution in the Jewish communities there.

Many Jewish villages were raided and hundreds of Jews were killed. Thousands decided to make their way to Israel, but the only way for them to leave Ethiopia was on foot, trekking hundreds of miles through the desert. Many did not survive the terrible journey.

Four Ethiopian Jews in their traditional clothing.

Many of the Ethiopian Jews who tried to escape to Israel had to walk hundreds of miles to reach freedom. Their journey was filled with many dangers. Can you help the Ethiopian Jews find their way to religious freedom in Israel?

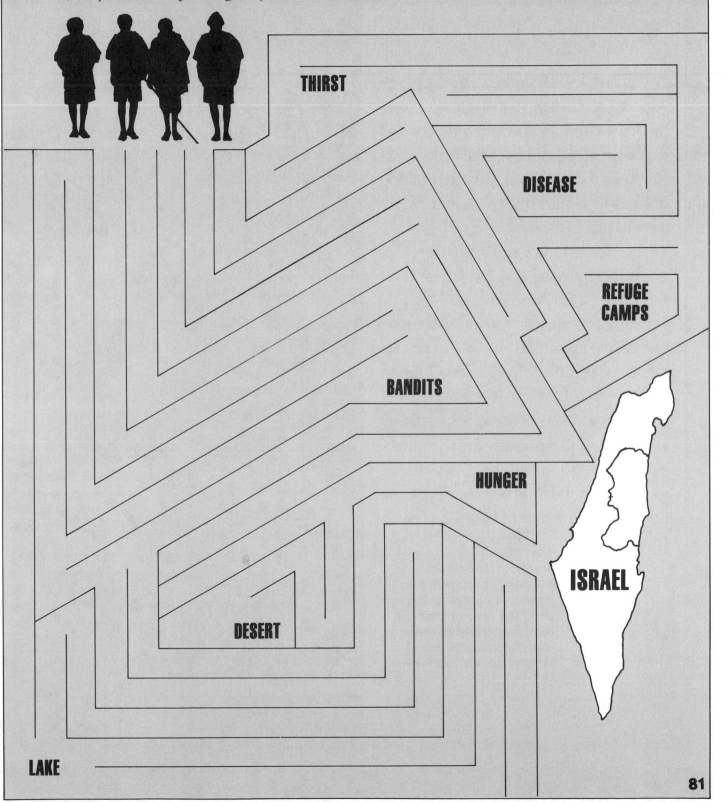

THIRST

DISEASE

REFUGE CAMPS

BANDITS

HUNGER

ISRAEL

DESERT

LAKE

OPERATION MOSES

The Jewish community in North America and in Israel acted quickly to save the Jews of Ethiopia. During a period of four short months in 1985, the United Jewish Appeal raised over sixty-two million dollars to send airplanes to take Ethiopian Jews to Israel.

This extraordinary airlift operation, organized by Israel and the Jewish community in North America, was called Operation Moses. Just as Moses led the Jewish people from slavery in Egypt, the modern Operation Moses rescued almost 8,000 Jews in Ethiopia! Yet thousands of Jews remain there. It is our responsibility to help them make their way to freedom. An organization called the American Association for Ethiopian Jews is leading the struggle to free all of Ethiopia's Jewish people.

An Ethiopian Jew sits outside her village home, weaving a basket. In the past, the Jews of Ethiopia lived in extreme poverty. Many have left Ethiopia for a better life in Israel.

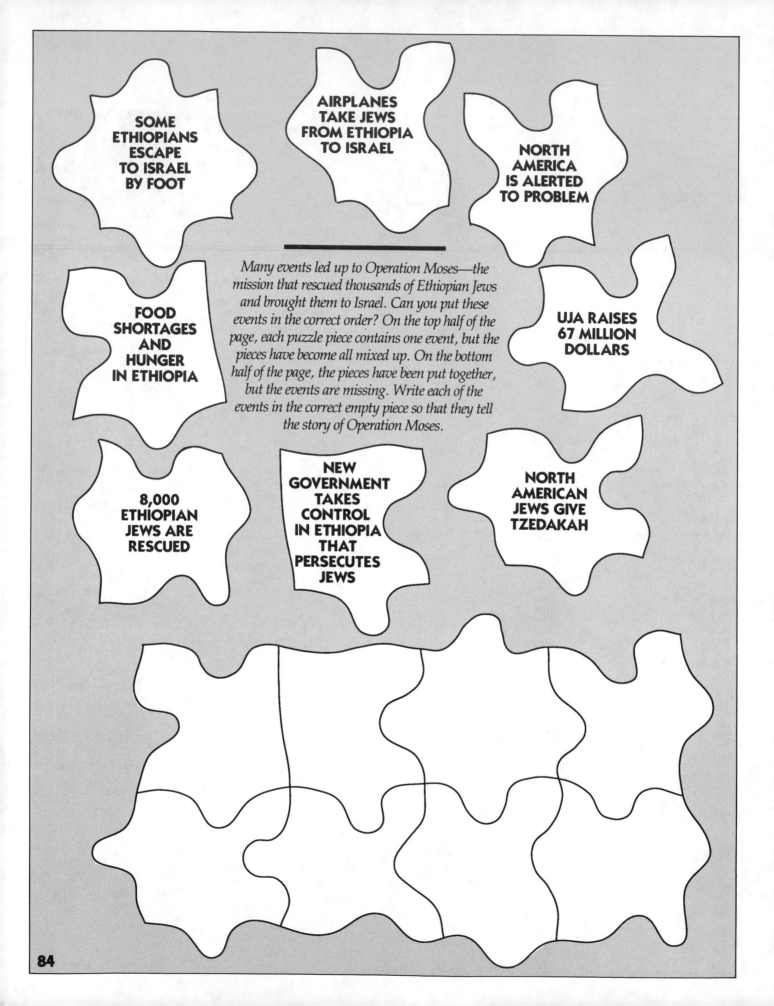

SOME ETHIOPIANS ESCAPE TO ISRAEL BY FOOT

AIRPLANES TAKE JEWS FROM ETHIOPIA TO ISRAEL

NORTH AMERICA IS ALERTED TO PROBLEM

FOOD SHORTAGES AND HUNGER IN ETHIOPIA

Many events led up to Operation Moses—the mission that rescued thousands of Ethiopian Jews and brought them to Israel. Can you put these events in the correct order? On the top half of the page, each puzzle piece contains one event, but the pieces have become all mixed up. On the bottom half of the page, the pieces have been put together, but the events are missing. Write each of the events in the correct empty piece so that they tell the story of Operation Moses.

UJA RAISES 67 MILLION DOLLARS

8,000 ETHIOPIAN JEWS ARE RESCUED

NEW GOVERNMENT TAKES CONTROL IN ETHIOPIA THAT PERSECUTES JEWS

NORTH AMERICAN JEWS GIVE TZEDAKAH

THE JEWISH COMMUNITY OF RUSSIA

Jews have lived in Russia for hundreds of years. Life was often very hard for the Jews in Russia. Discrimination and heavy taxes kept Russian Jewry very poor. Sometimes they were attacked by angry mobs. In these attacks, called pogroms, many Jews were beaten and killed, and their villages were destroyed.

In the late 1800s and early 1900s, 2.5 million Jews came to North America, many from Russia. Some of your immigrant ancestors probably came from there. But not all of the Russian Jews came to America. Many stayed behind. Things looked a little better for them after the Russian Revolution in 1917. The new Russian government promised to make life better for its citizens, including the Jews. But the promise was not kept. Although Russia has never been in favor of any religion, it has been particularly cruel to Judaism and to the Jewish people.

In recent days, Russia has become more tolerant. Jews no longer risk imprisonment or torture for teaching Hebrew and celebrating Jewish holidays. But problems remain. Even though Jews are now free to publicly practice Judaism without threats from the government, anti-Semitism is very prevalent. Anti-Semitic graffiti are painted on Jewish homes and buildings. Anger and hatred of the Jewish people still exist. Threats of violence and persecution continue. The severe economic problems of the last few years have increased ethnic tensions in Russia. In order to escape this tense and potentially dangerous situation, many Jews have tried to emigrate to America or to Israel.

Until recently, it was very difficult for Jews to leave Russia. Many Russian Jews lost their jobs and apartments, and some were arrested and sent to prison when they applied for a visa to leave the country. These Jews were called "refuseniks." During those difficult times before the government allowed Jews to emigrate freely to other countries, the number of Russian Jews arriving in Israel was as few as 1,000 a year. Today, it is much easier for Russian Jews to get permission from the government to emigrate. More than one million Russian Jews are expected to settle in Israel.

The Russian government made it very difficult for Jews to leave. Many Americans demonstrated against this unfair treatment of Jews, like these protesters in front of the Soviet Airline AEROFLOT.

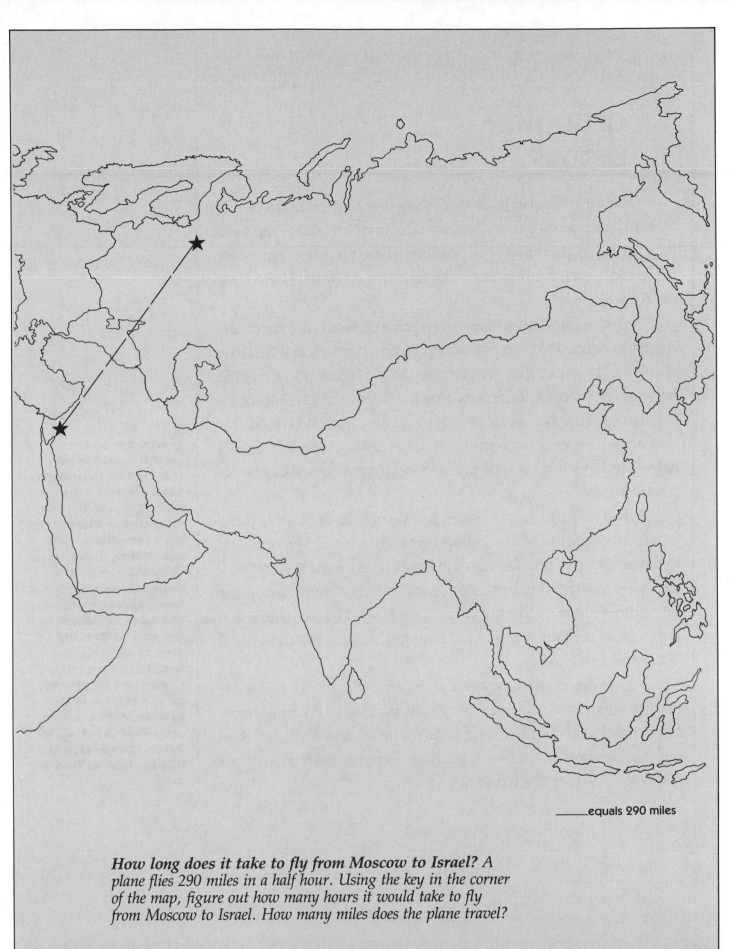

How long does it take to fly from Moscow to Israel? A plane flies 290 miles in a half hour. Using the key in the corner of the map, figure out how many hours it would take to fly from Moscow to Israel. How many miles does the plane travel?

equals 290 miles

OPERATION EXODUS

Because Russian Jews are coming in such great numbers, the State of Israel needs many new programs and services to help make their arrival as comfortable as possible. These programs have been undertaken with the help of special funds raised by the United Jewish Appeal.

Before the Russian Jews even arrive in Israel, a great deal of money is needed to help pay transportation costs. And when Russian Jews do arrive, they need a place to live. Classes to teach Hebrew are needed for these new Israelis. Often, the job skills of the Russian Jews are not useful in Israel, and they have to be trained in new areas. A special organization in Israel called the Jewish Agency helps the Jews from Russia and other foreign countries to be absorbed into Israeli society.

The effort to help Russian Jews emigrate to Israel is called Operation Exodus. Never before has such a large, vigorous and dynamic group of people arrived in Israel, determined to start a new life in the Jewish homeland. With Moscow just a three-hour plane ride from Tel Aviv, all of *klal yisrael* participate with great hope and joy as Israel continues to grow in strength and diversity as a result of this modern exodus.

Jews live in practically every country of the world, and some of them suffer hard lives of poverty and oppression. We must never forget our Jewish brothers and sisters who are less fortunate than we. As members of *klal yisrael,* we have a responsibility to help our fellow Jews all over the world.

Chava Carlin and her brother Yossi Shohet thought that they would never see each other again. Chava had emigrated to Israel at the age of seventeen while her brother, then nine years old, remained in Russia. Upon her arrival in Israel, Chava was trained as a nurse by Hadassah and worked for many years in a Hadassah hospital. It seemed that brother and sister would never meet. But in the summer of 1989, seventy years after Chava had left Russia, she was reunited with her brother Yossi in Israel.

TRUE AND FALSE CODE

Directions: Read each statement, decide if it is true or false, and circle the answer. Write the letter you circle under the correct box at the bottom of the page.

	TRUE	FALSE
1 There are about twenty million Jews living in Israel today	Y	A
2 There are about six million Jews living in the United States today	A	R
3 The Jews in Ethiopia are free to practice their Judaism	T	S
4 Most of the Jewish immigrants who came to America 100 years ago wanted to forget the communities they left behind in Europe	S	L
5 Six million Jews were victims of the Holocaust	L	E
6 One-fourth of the Jewish people in the world live in the State of Israel	R	Y
7 Operation Exodus helps Russian Jews emigrate to Israel	I	L
8 Zion is another name for Ethiopia	A	E
9 A person who believes that Jews should reestablish a homeland for themselves in *Eretz Yisrael* is a Zionist	L	M
10 Refuseniks are Jews who are not granted permission to leave Russia.	Y	B
11 All Jewish people, no matter where they live, belong to *klal Yisrael*	K	N

11	5	2	9		10	7	3	6	1	8	4

VI.
THE
JEWISH
COMMUNITY
AND YOU

THIS BOOK BEGAN
WITH HILLEL'S LESSON:

"If I am not for myself, who will be for me? But if I am for myself alone, what am I?"

As you studied the pages of this book, you learned the many ways we depend on each other. You learned how our Jewish community serves *klal yisrael,* the people of Israel. Each agency and organization in the community plays an important role in the life of the Jewish people.

Hillel's saying ends with a third line. It is this:

"And if not now, when?"

As you get older, there will be many ways you can contribute to *klal yisrael.* But Hillel asks why wait? The Jewish community needs your help now. This book has suggested many ways for you to participate. You can take part in the activities sponsored by your synagogue and Jewish community center. You can volunteer to help residents of the home for the aged. You can raise funds for the United Jewish Appeal. You can visit Israel. You can do many things, and you can do them now.

In the first chapter of this book, you learned that being part of the Jewish people is like being part of one big family. In a family, every member has certain responsibilities. In the same way, you, as a member of the Jewish community, have a role to play in keeping *klal yisrael* strong and healthy.

THE JEWISH COMMUNITY AND ME

Now that you have read about Jewish communities throughout the world, it is time to record some facts about yourself and your own Jewish community.

NAME _____

HOME ADDRESS

Street _____

City _____

State _____

Country _____

MY FAMILY

Mother's Name _____

Father's Name _____

Brothers _____

_____

Sisters _____

_____

Grandfathers _____

_____

Grandmothers _____

_____

SYNAGOGUE

Name _____

Street Address _____

City _____

State _____

Rabbi _____

Cantor _____

Principal _____

What subjects do you study at your synagogue? _____

_____

What organizations does the *tzedakah* you collect in class help?_____

_____

What activities does your synagogue sponsor for the community?_____

_____

THE JEWISH COMMUNITY CENTER

Do you belong to a JCC?_____

In what activities do you participate at the JCC?_____

_____

SUMMER CAMP

Do you go to a Jewish summer camp?

_____

Where is the camp?_____

_____

How many people go to camp?_____

_____

What do you do at the camp?_____

_____

How many weeks do you spend at camp?_____

_____

THE OLD AGE HOME

Have you ever visited an old age home?

_____

Who did you visit there?_____

_____

ISRAEL

Have you ever been to Israel?_____

_____

When did you visit _____ _____
                           (month)   (year)

What cities did you visit?_____

_____

Do you have any relatives living in Israel?_____

_____

What are their names and how are they related to you?_____

_____

Jewish Organizations I Belong To

_____

_____

Jewish Organizations My Family Belongs To

_____

_____

_____